# EVERYDAY CODING __

# GROUP PLANNING, CREATING, AND TESTING

## Programming Together

**Derek Miller**

Cavendish Square

New York

Published in 2018 by Cavendish Square Publishing, LLC
243 5th Avenue, Suite 136, New York, NY 10016

Library of Congress Cataloging-in-Publication Data

Names: Miller, Derek L., author.
Title: Group planning, creating, and testing: programming together / Derek L. Miller.
Description: New York : Cavendish Square Publishing, 2018. | Series: Everyday coding | Includes bibliographic references and index. | Audience: Grades 2-6. |
Identifiers: ISBN 9781502629937 (library bound) | ISBN 9781502629913 (pbk.) | ISBN 9781502629920 (6 pack) |ISBN 9781502629944 (ebook)
Subjects: LCSH: Computer programming--Juvenile literature. | Programming languages (Electronic computers)--Juvenile literature. | Computers--Juvenile literature.
Classification: LCC QA76.6 M547 2018 | DDC 005.1--dc23

Editorial Director: David McNamara
Editor: Caitlyn Miller
Copy Editor: Nathan Heidelberger
Associate Art Director: Amy Greenan
Designer: Christina Shults
Production Coordinator: Karol Szymczuk
Photo Research: J8 Media

Printed in the United States of America

# TABLE OF CONTENTS __

# Coding in Groups

**A**ny big project takes the hard work of a lot of people. Many fun activities need teams, too. Think of a soccer game. When players do their jobs well, they win games. Different players have different jobs. A team of goalies wouldn't win many games. A good soccer team needs all kinds of players. When people work as a team, they can accomplish a lot more. The same is true in **computer programming**.

*Opposite:* Popular games like Minecraft are made by teams of people.

Who do you think of when you hear the words "computer programming"? Most likely, you picture people like Steve Jobs and Bill Gates. They are famous around the world and have made billions of dollars. But they did not program all their ideas themselves. They created teams of people that helped them. It was these programmers who made the **programs** we use.

Group work is everywhere. People **collaborate** to come up with better ideas. Then, they put their ideas into action quicker by working together in groups. This happens every day around the world.

# CHAPTER 01

# A Closer Look at Group Programming

Have you ever done a group project? You probably have in school. Maybe your teacher had you design a car to go down a ramp. This is a common group project in many schools. You need to design your car to go as fast as possible. Then, every group tests their cars and sees just how fast they can go.

A group project like this has stages. It's often split into three stages: planning, creating, and testing. In the planning stage, group members

Working together can lead to great results, like a faster model car!

talk. They agree on what they want to do. Hopefully, they **improve** their ideas by collaborating. In the creating stage, the group makes the car. If any problems come up, they solve them together. In the testing stage, the group sees how well the car did. Then, they try to improve the design. Testing gives valuable information about what did or didn't work.

These three phases are also used in computer programming. Programs can do all sorts of things on computers and other **devices**. You've likely used programs like Microsoft Word to do homework. You've also probably used them for fun, like playing Minecraft.

All programs run using a **source code**. The code is a set of instructions telling the computer what to do. Programmers create programs by writing this code. That is why

Source code like this powers computer programs.

programmers are sometimes called coders.

The source code is like an instruction manual. It tells the program what to do and how to do it. Just like an instruction manual, any mistakes can create big problems. If a set of Legos comes with faulty instructions, it's really hard to put them together. This is why **coding** can be so hard. If one

person makes a mistake in the code, it can cause all sorts of **bugs**. Maybe the program won't run at all. Or maybe it

A program's source code is like a set of step-by-step instructions for building a Lego kit.

will just spit out the wrong results. This isn't a big deal if it is a program like Minecraft. But if it is a program to guide the path of a spaceship, you want it to work well!

These kinds of problems are why coding in groups is so great. It lets other people check your work, just like a partner in school. It is hard to see mistakes when you look at your own work. But when you look at your partner's work, it is easier to see problems. In coding, it is the same way. Programmers collaborate to help each other.

An early computer called the Mark I was so large that it needed its own room.

## Early Computers

Did you know that old computers were huge? Sixty years ago, one computer filled an entire room. They also couldn't do nearly as much as modern computers can today. Back then, bugs were caused by actual bugs. Insects could get stuck in the giant computers and make them stop working.

# CHAPTER 02

# Group Programming in Everyday Life

**H**ave you ever cooked with someone? Programming in a group is a lot like this. Imagine you are cooking a meal with your family. What is the first step? First of all, you need to decide what you are making. This is the group planning stage.

*Opposite:* Activities like cooking in a group are a lot like group programming.

In workplaces around the world, many people work together in groups.

Maybe you want to eat one thing, but your sibling wants to eat another. You need to work it out and decide what sounds best to everyone. Or you can decide to make both things! It all depends on how much time and food you have.

In programming, coders need to decide what they are trying to do. Maybe they are trying to make a cool new video game. Then, they need to decide what kind of game to make. If people have different ideas, they try to figure out the best one. If it's a business, they also need to look at which idea will make the most money. This is their group planning stage.

Mixing ingredients is often a job for just one person.

If you're making a meal, the creating stage is cooking it. Everyone in the group has a different role for this part. Maybe your job is to get the ingredients. Someone else is in charge of mixing them together. If everyone tries to mix a bowl full of food at the same time, it doesn't work. There's not enough room!

Graphic designers make sure a program or website looks good.

In coding, everyone has his or her own role, too. One coder might focus on making the **graphics** of a game. Another one might make the **sound effects**. A third will create the story that the game follows. Each role is important. Group members also have to make sure they each know what the other members are doing. If two people

Testing a product is an important step.

both make the sound effects, they end up wasting a lot of time.

In the testing stage, everyone tries the food that you cooked. If it tastes good, you are finished. But what if it tastes bad? Then, you can try to fix it. If you are lucky, it just needs more salt or sugar. That's easy to fix. If it's really bad, you might need to throw it out and start over again.

**Fatal Error** ☒

❌

OK

Testers try to find bugs so they can be fixed.

Coders also need to test their programs. They look for bugs that cause problems. When they find them, they can go to the source code and fix them. This process is called **debugging**. It is a lot easier in a group. Each programmer can check the work of the others. This makes it more likely they will find a bug.

Larry Page [*left*] and Sergey Brin [*right*], the founders of Google

# Google's Group

Many programs we use every day were made by groups of people. One of the most famous **tech companies** is Google. It was founded by two people working together in college, Larry Page and Sergey Brin. The two of them started Google together twenty years ago. Now Google has more than fifty thousand workers!

# CHAPTER 03

# Bringing It All Together

**W**orking in a group has many benefits. You can get a lot more work done in a group. More people means you do things faster than you can alone. It also means you can **brainstorm** and come up with better ideas. That's why collaboration is so popular in all kinds of businesses.

*Opposite:* Even kids can work together to make cool new programs.

Managers are like the coaches of sports teams. They decide who does what.

But working in a group also creates some difficulties. There needs to be a manager who keeps people on track. Everyone needs to have his or her own job in the group. If there's overlap, people might be working on the same thing. Too much overlap can waste time.

This is where another computer science idea fits in: **decomposition**. Decomposition is the

Making something out of papier-mâché takes many steps.

breaking down of a task into smaller parts. You use decomposition every day outside of coding. Think of when you do a large project in school. You have to break it down into smaller parts. Imagine you are making a **papier-mâché** globe in school. First, you tear a newspaper into pieces. Then, you dip them in glue. Next, you form the globe. Finally, you paint it.

Software testers look for bugs. Then, they write down any they find.

Group testing is one of the most important steps in programming. In fact, companies hire people whose only job is to test programs. They are called **software** testers. They see if they can "break" programs. If they can, the program is fixed so that the problem won't happen again.

Teachers check papers for errors, just as testers check programs for bugs.

Testing software is like your teacher checking your writing. Testers go through a checklist, just like some teachers do. The checklist makes sure they don't miss anything. They also **document** everything they find. This means they write down any issues that come up. Taking notes helps the programmers fix any problems. Your teacher also writes down any problems he or she finds in your

Video chatting
helps people
work together.

# Coding Around the World

One cool thing about programming in a group is that you can do it from anywhere. People from all around the globe work on projects together. One team member can be in the United States while another can be in Canada. This isn't a big deal because they can use the internet to talk to each other. This makes collaboration easy.

Working together can be a lot of fun!

writing. Your teacher's corrections help you fix any mistakes, too.

Creating new programs is a big job. Working in a group to plan and test helps. People bring different ideas to a project. And different people catch different mistakes. Finding ways to work well in a group is key. Working together is what makes important ideas a reality.

# GLOSSARY

**brainstorm**  To spend time thinking of new ideas.

**bugs**  Mistakes or errors in a computer program.

**coding**  Creating a computer program by writing the code that makes it run.

**collaborate**  To work together as a group or team.

**computer programming**  Another term for coding.

**debugging**  To find and fix errors in a program.

**decomposition**  The breaking down of a task into smaller parts.

**devices**  Electronic devices include cell phones and tablets.

**document**  To write down what happened.

**graphics** The images that a computer displays.

**improve** To make something better.

**papier-mâché** A material made of paper and glue used to make sculptures.

**programs** Computer instructions that accomplish a task. Some examples are Microsoft Word and Minecraft.

**software** Programs that run on computers and other devices.

**sound effects** The man-made sounds that video games and movies use.

**source code** The instructions that make computer programs run.

**tech companies** A company that focuses on technology. Some examples are Amazon, Google, and Facebook.

# FIND OUT MORE

## Books

McCue, Camille. *Getting Started with Coding: Get Creative with Code!* Hoboken, NJ: Wiley, 2015.

McManus, Sean. *How to Code in 10 Easy Lessons.* Irvine, CA: Walter Foster Jr., 2015.

## Websites

Coding for Kids 1: What is Computer Coding?

https://www.youtube.com/watch?v=THOEQ5soVpY

A video by DK Books explains computer programs.

CS Fundamentals: Debugging with the Step Button

https://www.youtube.com/watch?v=RUZTRNakV9c

Learn what debugging is and see an example of how to do it in Scratch, a programming language for kids.

# INDEX __

Page numbers in boldface
are illustrations.

**Derek Miller** is a teacher who writes about history and technology. He is the author of *Information and Action: Using Variables* and *Completing Tasks: Using Algorithms*. Derek likes to play computer games of all kinds.